Pudu D7 Robot
Intelligence in Motion – Everything You Need to Know

Behind the Scenes of a Semi-Humanoid Bot That Learns, Adapts, and Transforms the Workforce

Alejandro S. Diego

Table of Contents

Introduction...3

Chapter 1: The Evolution of Service Robots.............. 6

Chapter 2: Meet the Pudu D7 – Design and Structure 12

Chapter 3: Mobility and Precision – What Sets It Apart.. 20

Chapter 4: Arms of Intelligence – Advanced Movement Capabilities...27

Chapter 5: The AI-Powered Brain Behind the D7.... 34

Chapter 6: Real-World Applications of the Pudu D7... 42

Chapter 7: Efficiency and Cost-Effectiveness in Industry.. 51

Chapter 8: A Vision of the Future – Pudu's Roadmap 61

Chapter 9: Technical Mastery – The Engineering Behind the D7.. 72

Chapter 10: The Future of Human-Robot Collaboration.. 85

Conclusion.. 97

Introduction

AI-powered robots have rapidly transformed the landscape of technology and industry in recent years. What began as simple machines performing repetitive tasks has now evolved into intelligent systems capable of adapting and learning in real time. These robots are no longer confined to assembly lines or pre-programmed instructions; they are now integrated into various aspects of modern life, reshaping industries ranging from healthcare to hospitality. The rise of AI-driven robotics marks a significant shift in how we approach automation, with machines capable of performing complex tasks previously thought to require human intervention.

Among these innovations, the Pudu D7 robot stands out as a groundbreaking example of what semi-humanoid robots can achieve. Designed not only for functionality but also for adaptability, the Pudu D7 blends advanced AI with practical, human-like features. Unlike fully humanoid robots, which often face challenges in cost and implementation, the semi-humanoid design of the Pudu D7 strikes the perfect balance between efficiency and affordability. It is built to handle everything from delivering food in bustling restaurants to assisting patients in hospital corridors, all while learning and improving from each interaction. The robot's ability to adapt and evolve in dynamic environments has set a new standard for service automation.

Semi-humanoid robots like the Pudu D7 are playing a critical role in modern industries. As automation becomes more embedded in sectors such as retail, healthcare, and hospitality, the demand for robots that can interact naturally with their surroundings has never been higher. These robots don't just perform tasks; they are active participants in workflows, adapting to the challenges of real-world environments with remarkable precision. Their ability to navigate complex spaces, communicate with humans, and carry out a range of duties makes them indispensable in settings where flexibility and reliability are paramount.

The goal of this book is to delve deeply into the design, technology, and practical applications of the Pudu D7. We will explore how its semi-humanoid structure allows it to seamlessly integrate into human environments, the intelligence that drives its decision-making, and the industries where its impact is most profound. By breaking down the capabilities of the Pudu D7, we will uncover how this robot is not only advancing the field of service automation but also setting the stage for a future where intelligent machines are essential to everyday operations. Through this exploration, readers will gain a comprehensive understanding of the Pudu D7's potential to transform the workforce and redefine the role of robots in society.

Chapter 1: The Evolution of Service Robots

In the early days of robotics, service robots were largely task-specific, designed to carry out repetitive, predefined functions in controlled environments. These early machines were often found in manufacturing plants, where they performed simple, repetitive actions like welding or assembling parts. Their movements were entirely programmed, with little room for flexibility or adaptation. While efficient at their designated tasks, these robots were limited by their inability to react to changes in their surroundings or take on more complex roles that required decision-making or learning.

As industries began to demand more versatile machines, a shift occurred in the world of robotics. Instead of rigid, single-purpose robots, there was a growing interest in creating intelligent robots that could handle more dynamic environments. This shift was driven by advances in artificial intelligence and machine learning, which opened the door for robots to not only perform specific tasks but also learn from their experiences and adapt to new situations. These intelligent robots were no longer limited to a fixed set of instructions; they could analyze their environment, make decisions in real-time, and even improve their performance with each new task.

This evolution from task-specific to intelligent robots marked a critical turning point in the field of robotics. Industries like healthcare, hospitality, and retail, where environments are less predictable and require more human-like interaction, began to embrace these new robots. The development of AI-powered robots allowed for greater flexibility, enabling machines to navigate complex spaces, respond to human needs, and take on multiple roles without the need for constant reprogramming. This shift not only increased the efficiency of robots but also expanded their potential applications across a wide range of industries.

At the forefront of this revolution is the Pudu D7 robot, a prime example of how intelligent service robots are redefining automation. The Pudu D7 represents a new generation of robots, capable of learning, adapting, and performing a variety of tasks with precision and efficiency. With its advanced AI and semi-humanoid design, it serves as a bridge between the earlier task-specific robots and the fully intelligent machines that are becoming integral to modern industry. The shift towards intelligent robots like the Pudu D7 is not just a technological advancement; it signals a broader change in how we think about automation, human-robot collaboration, and the future of work.

The Pudu D7 perfectly embodies the evolution from task-specific robots to intelligent machines, seamlessly integrating into this rapidly advancing field. Unlike its predecessors, which were confined to fixed, repetitive roles, the Pudu D7 is designed to be highly adaptable, capable of functioning in dynamic environments where human interaction and situational flexibility are essential. Its semi-humanoid design is a reflection of this shift, as it borrows key features from human anatomy, such as arms and a torso, while maintaining a practical structure that enhances its efficiency in service-oriented industries. The Pudu D7's omnidirectional mobility, flexible arms, and intelligent learning system allow it to take on more complex tasks, making it a versatile tool in settings like hospitals, restaurants, and retail spaces.

At the heart of the Pudu D7's ability to adapt and perform a wide variety of tasks lies its integration of AI and machine learning. These technologies are what set it apart from older generations of robots. Instead of simply following pre-programmed instructions, the Pudu D7 utilizes AI to process vast amounts of data from its surroundings. It learns from every task it performs, every obstacle it encounters, and every interaction it has with humans. Over time, this continuous learning allows the robot to refine its performance, becoming more efficient and effective as it adapts to the nuances of its specific environment.

Machine learning plays a crucial role in this process. The Pudu D7 doesn't just execute commands; it improves its decision-making abilities with each new experience. For example, in a restaurant setting, the robot might learn how to navigate through a crowded space more efficiently after repeatedly moving through similar environments. In healthcare, it can adapt to the routines of hospital staff, understanding the most efficient routes to deliver supplies or assist patients. This learning capability significantly enhances the robot's value, allowing it to tackle a broader range of tasks while minimizing errors and increasing operational efficiency.

The development of robots like the Pudu D7, powered by AI and machine learning, marks a pivotal moment in robotics. These technologies enable robots to become more than just tools; they evolve into collaborative partners in the workforce, capable of making decisions and executing complex tasks that previously required human intervention. As industries continue to adopt AI-powered machines, the importance of these technologies in robot development becomes even more apparent. The ability of robots to learn, adapt, and improve over time is not just a feature—it's a necessity in today's fast-paced, ever-changing environments.

The Pudu D7, with its advanced AI systems, stands as a prime example of how robotics is evolving to meet the needs of modern industries. Its ability to blend machine learning with real-world applications ensures that it stays relevant and valuable as the landscape of work continues to shift toward automation. This robot is not just part of the evolutionary trend; it is at the forefront of it, setting the standard for what intelligent machines can achieve in the future of service and industry.

Chapter 2: Meet the Pudu D7 – Design and Structure

The Pudu D7 is a striking example of a semi-humanoid robot, designed with both practicality and adaptability in mind. Its purpose is to function in environments where human interaction and precision are crucial, making it a valuable asset across industries such as healthcare, hospitality, and retail. Unlike fully humanoid robots, which often face high production costs and implementation challenges, the semi-humanoid design of the Pudu D7 strikes a balance between human-like functionality and efficient performance. This approach allows it to blend into human environments with ease, performing tasks that require dexterity and mobility without the complexity of a fully human form.

Standing at 1.65 meters (5'4") and weighing around 45 kilograms (100 pounds), the Pudu D7 is built to move seamlessly through spaces designed for human workers. Its upper body, designed to resemble a human torso and arms, is one of its most defining features. This semi-humanoid structure allows the robot to interact naturally with objects and people, using its arms to handle tasks that require flexibility and precision. The arms themselves are about 65 centimeters long, giving the robot just enough reach to perform duties such as delivering meals, handling fragile items, or assisting with logistics in busy environments.

The Pudu D7's omnidirectional wheelbase is a key feature that enhances its mobility. Unlike traditional wheeled robots that move in a straight line, the Pudu D7 can rotate 360 degrees and navigate tight or crowded spaces with high precision. This capability is especially useful in environments like restaurants, where maneuvering through narrow aisles or avoiding obstacles is crucial. The robot's wheels are not just for smooth movement—they allow for seamless transitions in direction without requiring the robot to fully turn its body. This level of agility enables the Pudu D7 to maintain the flow of human activity around it, ensuring that it moves efficiently without causing disruptions.

One of the standout features of the Pudu D7 is its adaptable arms. Each arm offers 30 degrees of freedom, allowing the robot to perform a wide range of motions, from simple lifting tasks to more complex manipulations. These arms are not static; depending on the task at hand, they can be equipped with various attachments, including human-like hands. In its most advanced configuration, the robot's hands can have up to 20 degrees of freedom, which significantly increases its dexterity. This flexibility makes the Pudu D7 capable of handling delicate objects, picking up items, and interacting with its surroundings in ways that traditional robots cannot. This adaptability is what sets it apart in environments where precision and human-like handling are essential.

The design of the Pudu D7 goes beyond aesthetics—it's a functional tool built to interact in spaces traditionally occupied by humans. Its semi-humanoid form and omnidirectional mobility are essential in allowing it to work in environments where both space and interaction require careful navigation. The robot's ability to adapt its arms and use attachments like humanoid hands means it can handle a variety of tasks that demand both strength and precision. These features not only make the Pudu D7 versatile but also crucial in sectors where efficiency, adaptability, and interaction are paramount to success.

The design of the Pudu D7 is specifically crafted to excel in environments where navigation through tight spaces and dealing with complex surroundings are critical. This is particularly important in settings like restaurants, hospitals, and retail spaces, where the robot must move fluidly among people and objects. Its omnidirectional wheelbase allows it to maneuver with remarkable precision, enabling it to pivot and change direction smoothly without needing to fully turn its body. This capability is a significant advantage in areas with narrow aisles, busy corridors, or crowded rooms where every inch of space counts.

The robot's compact size and its ability to make quick adjustments in movement ensure it can function seamlessly without disrupting human activities. For example, in a restaurant, the Pudu D7 can navigate between tables and around patrons while carrying trays of food, without causing any delays or disturbances. Similarly, in a hospital setting, the robot can move through hallways and patient rooms, delivering supplies or assisting staff, all while avoiding obstacles and maintaining a consistent pace. Its ability to navigate in environments where space is limited is a key factor that sets the Pudu D7 apart from more rigid service robots.

When compared to other service robots, the Pudu D7 stands out due to its combination of agility, adaptability, and intelligent design. Traditional service robots, such as those used for simple food delivery or cleaning, are often confined to linear movements or require extensive pre-programming to operate in specific environments. These robots might be effective at performing singular tasks, but they lack the flexibility to handle dynamic environments or interact fluidly with humans. The Pudu D7, however, can adapt on the fly, making adjustments in real-time to account for changes in its surroundings. This ability to react and adapt makes it far more versatile in industries where conditions can shift rapidly.

Additionally, many existing service robots are either task-specific or heavily reliant on human intervention for programming and operation. For example, a robot designed for cleaning may be highly effective in that role but unable to perform other tasks or adapt to unexpected changes in its environment. In contrast, the Pudu D7 is built to handle multiple functions, from delivering items to interacting with customers, all while learning and improving over time. Its semi-humanoid design allows it to perform tasks that require a level of dexterity and interaction that simpler, more task-specific robots cannot achieve.

Another key difference is the Pudu D7's focus on human-robot interaction. While many service robots are designed to work behind the scenes, often out of sight, the Pudu D7 is intended to actively engage with people, whether by delivering meals, assisting patients, or providing support in retail environments. Its human-like form, equipped with flexible arms and hands, enables it to bridge the gap between purely mechanical tools and more interactive machines. This makes it more suitable for roles where communication and engagement with humans are vital, such as customer service or healthcare support.

The Pudu D7's advanced design for navigating tight spaces, combined with its adaptability and interaction capabilities, makes it a clear frontrunner in the evolution of service robots. While other robots may excel in specific tasks, the

D7's ability to move with precision, handle complex environments, and engage directly with people places it in a category of its own, offering solutions that are both practical and innovative for a wide range of industries.

Chapter 3: Mobility and Precision – What Sets It Apart

The Pudu D7's advanced omnidirectional movement is one of its defining features, allowing it to navigate through complex environments with unmatched precision. This movement capability enables the robot to rotate 360 degrees, making it highly agile in confined spaces where sharp turns or immediate adjustments are necessary. Unlike traditional robots that often require wide arcs to change direction, the Pudu D7 can pivot in place, which is essential in environments such as busy restaurant kitchens, hospital corridors, or crowded retail floors. Its ability to move smoothly in any direction means it can navigate around obstacles, whether stationary or moving, without disrupting the workflow around it.

This advanced mobility is not just about fluidity in movement—it also contributes significantly to the robot's overall speed and efficiency. The Pudu D7 is designed to maintain the pace of human activity, operating at a top speed of 2 meters per second, or roughly 7.2 kilometers per hour. This speed allows the robot to keep up with the natural flow of activity in fast-paced settings, such as restaurants during peak hours or hospitals where time-sensitive tasks are critical. Whether it's delivering meals or transporting medical supplies, the D7 ensures that it operates at a pace that matches human workers, reducing delays and increasing overall productivity.

What sets the Pudu D7 apart from many other service robots is its ability to handle not only flat surfaces but also more challenging terrains. The robot is designed to navigate slopes of up to 10 degrees, making it adaptable to environments where level changes are common, such as ramps in hospitals or uneven surfaces in industrial spaces. This feature adds to the robot's versatility, allowing it to maintain stability and balance even when moving across varied terrains. Its ability to adjust to different surfaces ensures that it can perform consistently in a wide range of environments, providing smooth operation regardless of the floor plan or terrain type.

In confined spaces where every inch of movement matters, the Pudu D7 excels by combining speed, precision, and versatility. Its omnidirectional movement allows it to avoid obstacles and maneuver through tight areas without having to constantly recalibrate its position. Whether it's weaving through a busy kitchen or navigating a bustling hospital ward, the robot can adapt to the situation and keep pace with the human activity around it. The combination of its advanced movement technology, speed, and ability to handle diverse terrains makes the Pudu D7 a highly efficient solution in industries that demand both agility and reliability.

By addressing these critical aspects of mobility, the Pudu D7 is designed to not just move efficiently but to integrate seamlessly into environments where space and time are often limited. Its ability to maneuver through confined spaces with precision, maintain speed in fast-paced settings, and handle varied terrains makes it an indispensable tool in service industries that require flexibility and efficiency from their robotic counterparts.

The Pudu D7 is designed not only for agility but also for high-precision tasks, making it an incredibly versatile tool across various industries. One of its standout features is its ability to lift objects up to 10 kilograms with a remarkable accuracy of 0.1 millimeters. This level of precision ensures that the robot can handle delicate and potentially fragile items without the risk of damage, making it ideal for environments where careful handling is essential. Whether it's transporting medical supplies in a hospital or delicately arranging food items in a restaurant, the Pudu D7's precision is a key factor that enhances its effectiveness.

In real-world applications, the Pudu D7's precision is invaluable, especially in settings where accuracy and consistency are critical. In restaurant kitchens, for example, the robot can seamlessly carry trays of food or drink, delivering them to tables without the risk of spillage or mishandling. The robot's ability to lift and transport items accurately, combined with its precise mobility, ensures that service flows smoothly, even in fast-paced environments. This allows restaurant staff to focus on more complex tasks, while the Pudu D7 handles the repetitive work of serving food and beverages with consistency and care.

In hospitals, where precision can have life-or-death implications, the Pudu D7's capabilities are even more impactful. The robot can transport medical supplies, medication, or sensitive equipment, ensuring they arrive exactly where they're needed, without human error or delays. Its precision in handling objects becomes crucial when dealing with fragile medical equipment or items that need to be transported with exact care. Furthermore, in high-stress environments like emergency rooms or operating theaters, the Pudu D7's ability to deliver critical supplies accurately and swiftly can make a substantial difference in the efficiency of healthcare operations.

The ability to lift up to 10 kilograms, combined with its omnidirectional movement, allows the Pudu D7 to perform tasks that go beyond simple transportation. It can assist in industrial settings, moving goods in warehouses or helping with stocking shelves in retail environments, all while maintaining the same high level of precision. In these spaces, where both mobility and careful handling are required, the robot's capacity to carry out tasks with such accuracy becomes an asset that streamlines operations, reduces errors, and increases productivity.

By blending its precise lifting abilities with its advanced movement capabilities, the Pudu D7 is equipped to handle a variety of tasks in environments that demand both strength and finesse. Its ability to lift and transport items with pinpoint accuracy makes it suitable for industries where handling fragile, sensitive, or valuable items is a regular occurrence. This high level of precision, coupled with its agility, makes the Pudu D7 not just a tool for basic service work but a powerful asset in environments that rely on accuracy and efficiency to function smoothly.

Chapter 4: Arms of Intelligence – Advanced Movement Capabilities

One of the key features that set the Pudu D7 apart from many other service robots is the flexibility of its arms, which are designed with 30 degrees of freedom. This allows the robot to carry out complex tasks that require intricate movements and precise control. The degrees of freedom enable the arms to move in multiple directions, mimicking the range of motion found in human limbs. This flexibility is essential for tasks that go beyond basic lifting or carrying, such as interacting with objects that require fine manipulation or handling tasks that demand careful dexterity.

The Pudu D7's arms are not static; they can be outfitted with various attachments depending on the task at hand. These attachments range from simple tools for carrying or pushing objects to more sophisticated, human-like hands capable of detailed manipulation. The ability to swap attachments means the robot can easily adapt to different environments and duties. For example, in its most advanced configuration, the Pudu D7 can be equipped with humanoid hands that offer up to 20 degrees of freedom. This brings an added layer of dexterity, enabling the robot to handle more delicate or complex tasks, such as picking up small objects, adjusting equipment, or interacting with fragile materials.

In service environments like hospitals or retail settings, this adaptability is invaluable. With humanoid hands, the Pudu D7 can perform tasks that require precision, such as assisting in the handling of medical instruments or stocking delicate items on shelves. In contrast, for environments that demand more straightforward actions, such as transporting goods or delivering items, simpler attachments may be used. This flexibility allows the robot to transition between various roles, making it highly versatile across different industries.

The ability to configure the arms with different attachments also means that the Pudu D7 can be tailored to the specific needs of any given task or environment. This not only enhances its efficiency but also reduces the need for specialized robots for each individual function. By integrating the capacity for multiple configurations, the Pudu D7 proves itself as a multifunctional asset capable of adapting to a wide array of tasks without the need for extensive reprogramming or additional machinery.

In environments where robots must perform a variety of roles, the Pudu D7's flexible arms and interchangeable attachments give it a distinct advantage. Whether it's handling intricate tasks with humanoid hands or performing more robust functions with simple tools, the robot's adaptability ensures that it can meet the demands of any situation. This ability to flexibly switch between configurations makes the Pudu D7 a versatile solution in settings where both precision and versatility are key.

The Pudu D7's dexterity is one of its most remarkable features, allowing it to handle a variety of practical tasks with precision. Its ability to manage delicate objects and manipulate small items makes it invaluable in industries where careful handling is essential. In healthcare settings, for instance, the Pudu D7 can assist with the transport and placement of fragile medical supplies or instruments, reducing the risk of human error or accidental damage. Whether it's handling vials of medication, surgical tools, or delicate equipment, the robot's precise movements ensure that tasks are carried out safely and efficiently, without the risk of dropping or mishandling sensitive items.

In retail environments, this dexterity is equally important. The Pudu D7 can be used to stock shelves, particularly in areas where small or fragile goods are displayed. Its ability to manipulate items with care means it can handle anything from fragile electronics to glassware, ensuring that these items are placed on shelves without causing damage. This allows human workers to focus on more complex tasks, while the robot takes care of the repetitive and delicate processes involved in handling merchandise.

The hospitality industry also benefits significantly from the Pudu D7's dexterity. In busy restaurants, for example, the robot can carry trays of food or beverages and deliver them directly to tables, all while maintaining the stability and care needed to prevent spills or breakages. This level of precision in service not only increases efficiency but also enhances the customer experience by ensuring consistent and reliable delivery. The Pudu D7 can also be used in hotels for tasks such as delivering room service or assisting with luggage, again leveraging its ability to handle items with care and precision.

The significance of the Pudu D7's dexterity extends beyond just handling objects—it is a critical factor in its ability to adapt to various roles within different industries. In healthcare, where accuracy is paramount, the robot's ability to move precisely and handle delicate instruments ensures that critical tasks are performed without error. In retail, its dexterity allows it to interact with a wide range of products, from small trinkets to valuable electronics, with the same level of care. In hospitality, the robot's ability to seamlessly integrate into service roles that require both speed and care makes it a valuable tool for improving operational efficiency.

Dexterity in robots like the Pudu D7 is not just a feature; it's a necessity in environments where human-robot collaboration is key. In industries where errors can be costly or even dangerous, the Pudu D7's ability to perform complex tasks with precision reduces risk and improves overall workflow. Whether it's assisting in surgeries, stocking shelves, or delivering meals, the Pudu D7's practical use of dexterity showcases its versatility and value across various sectors. Its ability to handle delicate and small items with such care positions it as an essential asset in modern industries that require both reliability and finesse.

Chapter 5: The AI-Powered Brain Behind the D7

The Pudu D7 robot's capabilities are rooted in its sophisticated multi-layered intelligence system, which seamlessly combines data-driven intelligence with advanced AI technology. This system allows the robot to move beyond basic automation and into the realm of true adaptability and learning. Instead of simply following pre-programmed instructions, the Pudu D7 analyzes its environment in real-time, making decisions based on the data it collects through each interaction. By integrating multiple layers of intelligence, the robot can perform a range of tasks with increasing efficiency and precision, learning as it goes to enhance its performance over time.

At the core of the Pudu D7's functionality is artificial intelligence, which plays a crucial role in its ability to adapt to dynamic environments. Unlike older generations of service robots that were limited to fixed roles and repetitive tasks, the Pudu D7 uses

AI to process vast amounts of data collected from its surroundings. This data-driven approach allows the robot to not only understand its environment but also make informed decisions on how to navigate and interact within it. Whether it's identifying obstacles, determining the most efficient route in a busy setting, or understanding how to carry out complex tasks, AI enables the Pudu D7 to function autonomously and intelligently.

This ability to learn from its environment is what sets the Pudu D7 apart from traditional service robots. With each new task or interaction, the robot refines its decision-making process, becoming more adept at recognizing patterns and responding to unique challenges. For example, in a restaurant setting, the Pudu D7 might learn how to adjust its movements to avoid collisions during peak dining hours or optimize its tray handling for more efficient service. In a hospital, the robot could adapt to the routines of staff, learning which corridors to avoid during high-traffic periods or how to adjust its speed when carrying delicate medical supplies.

The real-time adaptability of the Pudu D7 is one of its most powerful attributes. Each interaction it has, whether with an object, a person, or a physical space, is logged and used to improve its future performance. This constant feedback loop allows the robot to become smarter and more efficient as it gathers more experience. Over time, the Pudu D7 doesn't just perform tasks—it learns how to perform them better. This capability is especially valuable in industries like healthcare and hospitality, where environments can change rapidly and the robot must be able to adjust its behavior on the fly.

By combining data-driven intelligence with AI, the Pudu D7 can make real-time decisions that enhance its ability to function in complex environments. Its learning ability enables it to adapt to the nuances of different settings, whether that means adjusting its path in a crowded restaurant or refining its grip to handle fragile medical supplies. This constant learning process ensures that the Pudu D7 evolves alongside the tasks it performs, becoming more accurate, efficient, and reliable with each new experience.

The Pudu D7's multi-layered intelligence system, paired with its ability to learn and adapt, positions it as a highly capable tool in industries where flexibility and precision are essential. This combination of AI and data-driven intelligence doesn't just make the robot a passive participant in its environment—it transforms it into an active, evolving component of the workforce, constantly improving and adjusting to meet the demands of the modern world.

The Pudu D7's multi-layered intelligence system enables it to take on a wide range of practical tasks, making it a versatile tool across various industries. In a restaurant setting, for example, the robot can serve food by navigating through crowded spaces with precision, delivering trays of meals to customers without disturbing the flow of human activity. Its omnidirectional movement and precise handling allow it to carry items without spilling or damaging them, ensuring a smooth dining experience. This ability to efficiently move through busy environments also makes the Pudu D7 invaluable in retail spaces, where it can transport goods or restock shelves, freeing up human staff to focus on more customer-centric tasks.

In hospitals, the Pudu D7 plays an even more crucial role, assisting with the transportation of medical supplies, equipment, or medications. The robot's precision and reliability ensure that these items reach their destination safely, reducing the potential for human error and freeing up healthcare workers to focus on more urgent matters. Whether it's delivering medication to patient rooms or transporting fragile medical instruments, the Pudu D7 helps streamline hospital operations by taking over routine yet critical tasks.

These practical applications are made possible by the Pudu D7's intelligent control system, which operates on both high-level and low-level planning. High-level control involves strategic decision-making, such as determining the best route to take when delivering food in a restaurant or figuring out the most efficient way to transport goods through a hospital. This type of planning allows the robot to analyze its environment and make decisions that optimize its overall performance. High-level control is essential in environments where conditions are constantly changing, and the robot must be able to adapt its broader strategy to ensure smooth operation.

Low-level control, on the other hand, handles the real-time execution of tasks. This includes adjusting its grip on an object, navigating around obstacles, or avoiding sudden changes in its environment. For example, if the Pudu D7 is delivering food in a restaurant and someone steps into its path, the low-level control system will instantly adjust its movement to avoid a collision. Similarly, if the robot is transporting medical supplies and detects an obstacle in a hospital corridor, it will recalibrate its route in real-time to ensure that it continues its task without interruption. Low-level control ensures that the robot can respond to immediate challenges while maintaining the overall goals set by high-level planning.

A practical example of high-level control in action would be the Pudu D7 assessing a busy restaurant during peak hours and determining the most efficient path to deliver food without disturbing patrons. It may strategically choose a route that avoids high-traffic areas or tables where guests are more likely to be getting up from their seats. At the same time, its low-level control ensures that if an unexpected obstacle, like a dropped item or a sudden crowd, appears in its way, it can adjust its speed, change direction, or maneuver around the obstacle without requiring any external intervention.

In a hospital, high-level control might involve determining the most efficient sequence of deliveries for medical supplies based on urgency or room locations. The robot could decide which items to deliver first, optimizing its route for speed and minimizing delays between deliveries. Meanwhile, the low-level control ensures that the robot can handle tight corridors, sudden obstacles like moving hospital beds, or people crossing its path, all while maintaining the integrity of the items it's transporting.

This combination of high-level strategic planning and low-level real-time responsiveness gives the Pudu D7 a unique ability to function autonomously in complex environments. Its ability to plan broadly while making on-the-fly adjustments in real-time ensures that it remains efficient and reliable, even in the most dynamic settings. Whether serving food in a busy restaurant or assisting with critical tasks in a hospital, the Pudu D7's dual control planning system allows it to perform its duties with both foresight and precision.

Chapter 6: Real-World Applications of the Pudu D7

The Pudu D7 has found a natural home in the hospitality industry, where its advanced capabilities are redefining tasks like food delivery, guest interaction, and general hotel assistance. In restaurants, for example, the Pudu D7's ability to navigate busy dining areas with precision and speed makes it an ideal server. It can carry multiple trays of food and beverages, delivering them directly to tables without the risk of spillage or disturbing customers. This efficiency reduces the burden on human staff, allowing them to focus on customer service, order management, and more complex tasks. The robot's precision and reliability help streamline service during peak dining hours, ensuring that orders are delivered quickly and accurately.

Beyond food delivery, the Pudu D7 also plays a role in guest interaction within hospitality settings like hotels. It can assist with routine tasks such as delivering room service, toiletries, or luggage directly to guests' rooms. The robot's semi-humanoid design, combined with its ability to learn from each interaction, ensures that it can adapt to different tasks while maintaining a high standard of service. Its presence also adds a touch of futuristic innovation to the guest experience, enhancing customer satisfaction while providing practical, hands-on assistance. By handling these routine tasks, the Pudu D7 allows hotel staff to focus on creating a more personalized and engaging experience for guests, improving overall operational efficiency.

In the healthcare industry, the Pudu D7 is equally transformative, particularly in environments where precision, reliability, and speed are crucial. Hospitals are fast-paced, often chaotic places where timely delivery of medical supplies, equipment, and medications can make a significant difference in patient care. The Pudu D7's ability to transport these items swiftly and safely across hospital corridors ensures that essential materials reach their destinations without delay. By taking over these routine but critical tasks, the robot frees up healthcare professionals to focus on direct patient care and more complex medical procedures.

Additionally, the Pudu D7 plays a valuable role in assisting patients, especially in long-term care or rehabilitation settings. Its ability to deliver items such as medication, meals, or personal care products directly to patient rooms minimizes the need for staff to perform repetitive delivery tasks. This not only improves the efficiency of the hospital's operations but also ensures that patients receive the care they need in a timely manner. The robot's precise movement through narrow corridors and ability to navigate around obstacles like beds and medical carts further enhances its utility in hospital environments.

Navigating hospital corridors can be particularly challenging, but the Pudu D7 is equipped with advanced sensors and AI-driven learning systems that allow it to adapt to its surroundings. Its omnidirectional movement ensures it can travel smoothly through busy hallways, adjusting to the presence of people, medical equipment, and other obstacles. The robot's ability to handle these real-time challenges makes it a valuable asset in hospitals, where the flow of movement and the timely delivery of supplies are critical to daily operations. Whether it's delivering medication, assisting with logistics, or ensuring sterile supplies are transported safely, the Pudu D7 helps streamline hospital workflows and reduce human error.

In both hospitality and healthcare, the Pudu D7's ability to combine efficient service with real-time adaptability ensures it plays a vital role in improving operational workflows. Its precision in handling objects, ability to interact naturally with humans, and capability to adapt to varying environments makes it a practical and innovative solution in industries that require both reliability and flexibility. Whether serving meals in a restaurant or assisting medical staff in a hospital, the Pudu D7 enhances efficiency and allows human workers to focus on tasks that demand more specialized skills, ultimately improving overall service quality in both industries.

In the retail industry, the Pudu D7 robot is revolutionizing how businesses manage their daily operations. One of the most practical applications of the robot in this setting is its ability to stock shelves efficiently and with precision. Whether it's placing fragile items like electronics or restocking fast-moving consumer goods, the Pudu D7 can handle a wide variety of products. Its ability to lift up to 10 kilograms with precise control ensures that items are placed carefully and consistently on shelves, reducing the risk of damage. This not only helps streamline the restocking process but also allows human staff to focus on more customer-facing roles, improving the overall customer experience.

The Pudu D7's role in assisting customers is another significant advantage for retail environments. Its semi-humanoid design allows it to interact with customers in a way that feels natural, offering assistance such as guiding them to specific products or even providing real-time inventory updates. This interaction adds a futuristic, tech-driven element to the shopping experience, while also reducing the strain on human staff during peak shopping hours. By managing routine inquiries and basic customer interactions, the Pudu D7 helps create a smoother, more efficient shopping experience for both customers and employees.

One of the standout features of the Pudu D7 in retail is its ability to handle unexpected scenarios. Retail environments can be unpredictable, with sudden changes in customer flow, shifting stock needs, or obstacles in the aisles. The Pudu D7's advanced AI and real-time adaptability allow it to adjust its tasks and movements accordingly. For example, if a busy shopping aisle becomes blocked by customers or a temporary display, the robot can autonomously recalibrate its route to avoid delays. This ability to navigate complex, dynamic environments without human intervention makes the Pudu D7 a valuable tool in maintaining retail operations smoothly, even in unpredictable circumstances.

Looking beyond retail, the potential future applications of the Pudu D7 extend into a variety of industries, particularly warehouses and logistics. In warehouses, the need for efficient movement of goods is critical, and the Pudu D7's precision and load-carrying capability make it an ideal candidate for automating tasks such as inventory management, order picking, and goods transportation. Its ability to handle heavy loads with accuracy, combined with its adaptability in navigating warehouse environments, makes it a valuable asset for improving productivity and reducing human labor in these high-demand spaces.

In the logistics industry, the Pudu D7 could be used to assist with the movement and sorting of goods in distribution centers. Its ability to learn from its surroundings and adapt in real-time would allow it to efficiently transport packages, sort items based on delivery priority, or assist with packaging tasks. As the demand for faster, more efficient logistics solutions continues to grow, the Pudu D7's combination of AI-driven adaptability and precision handling positions it as an essential tool in optimizing supply chain processes.

Beyond these industries, the Pudu D7 holds potential for roles in sectors such as hospitality logistics, manufacturing, and even more niche environments like airports or museums. Its ability to adapt to different environments, combined with its flexible arms and configurable attachments, makes it suitable for a wide range of tasks, from guiding visitors in public spaces to handling delicate equipment in industrial settings. As more industries adopt automation, the Pudu D7's multi-functional design and real-time adaptability could be leveraged in an ever-expanding array of roles, offering solutions for businesses looking to streamline their operations.

In all of these applications, the Pudu D7's ability to handle both routine and unexpected tasks ensures that it remains a valuable asset across a broad spectrum of industries. Its capacity to adapt to new environments and learn from its interactions makes it well-suited for a future where automation and AI-driven robotics are central to industrial and commercial success.

Chapter 7: Efficiency and Cost-Effectiveness in Industry

The Pudu D7 plays a pivotal role in helping businesses reduce operational costs by automating repetitive and physically demanding tasks. One of the primary ways it achieves this is by taking over tasks that typically require significant human labor, such as delivering food in restaurants, transporting goods in hospitals, or restocking shelves in retail environments. By automating these tasks, companies can reduce the number of human workers needed for routine jobs, which leads to lower labor costs, fewer human errors, and increased efficiency.

In settings like restaurants, where staffing during peak hours can be expensive and difficult to manage, the Pudu D7 offers a cost-effective solution. It can handle food delivery and service, allowing restaurant staff to focus on more complex tasks such as customer interaction or meal preparation. This reduction in labor-intensive duties not only saves on staffing costs but also minimizes the risk of human error, such as incorrect orders or delayed service. The robot's ability to operate continuously without the need for breaks ensures that service is uninterrupted, further boosting overall productivity.

In healthcare, the Pudu D7 reduces operational costs by taking over tasks that typically require manual labor, such as transporting medical supplies or equipment across hospital floors. These tasks are repetitive yet essential, and having human staff handle them can lead to inefficiencies, especially in a busy hospital environment where time is crucial. By automating the delivery of supplies, the Pudu D7 ensures that items are transported quickly and accurately, reducing the time and cost associated with manual transport. Hospitals can then allocate their human staff to more critical roles, such as patient care, improving overall operational efficiency while cutting down on labor expenses.

Similarly, in retail environments, the Pudu D7 takes on physically demanding tasks like stocking shelves or moving goods. These activities often require multiple workers and can be time-consuming, especially in larger stores. By automating the restocking process, the Pudu D7 helps retailers optimize their workforce, allowing them to reduce the number of employees needed for inventory management. The robot's ability to handle these repetitive tasks means that stores can operate more efficiently, reducing the costs associated with labor while improving the speed and accuracy of stocking shelves.

The Pudu D7's durability and ability to work long hours without breaks or fatigue further enhance its cost-saving potential. Unlike human employees, the robot can operate for extended periods, reducing the need for multiple shifts or overtime pay. Additionally, its precision and ability to learn from its environment reduce the likelihood of mistakes that can lead to costly errors, such as misplaced inventory or incorrect deliveries. By consistently performing tasks accurately and efficiently, the Pudu D7 minimizes waste and operational inefficiencies, leading to long-term cost reductions for businesses.

Another key benefit of automation with the Pudu D7 is the reduction in workplace injuries. Many of the tasks the robot takes on, such as lifting heavy items or navigating through tight spaces, can be physically demanding and prone to accidents when performed by humans. By replacing these physically strenuous tasks with automation, businesses can reduce the risk of employee injuries, which in turn decreases the costs associated with workers' compensation, healthcare, and lost productivity due to injury-related absences. This not only enhances the safety of the workplace but also contributes to significant savings in operational expenses.

Overall, the Pudu D7's ability to automate repetitive and physically demanding tasks leads to a more streamlined and cost-effective operation. Whether in hospitality, healthcare, or retail, the robot allows businesses to reduce labor costs, improve efficiency, and enhance the accuracy and reliability of their services. By incorporating the Pudu D7 into their operations, companies can focus their human workforce on higher-level tasks that require creativity and problem-solving, while the robot handles the routine work, creating a balanced and productive environment.

By taking over repetitive and physically demanding tasks, the Pudu D7 enables human workers to shift their focus to more strategic, value-added roles. This shift not only improves overall efficiency but also enhances job satisfaction, as employees are freed from routine tasks and can engage in more creative or problem-solving activities that require human insight and interaction. For example, in a restaurant, instead of focusing on delivering food to tables, human staff can spend more time interacting with customers, managing orders, and ensuring that guests have a personalized experience. Similarly, in healthcare settings, medical staff can concentrate on providing patient care rather than being tied up with the transportation of supplies or equipment.

The Pudu D7 creates a more balanced and efficient workflow by managing the routine tasks that often consume valuable time and resources. This allows human workers to be deployed in areas where their skills and expertise are most needed, such as decision-making, customer service, or innovation. In retail, for instance, rather than being tasked with restocking shelves or organizing products, workers can focus on improving customer experiences, advising shoppers, or managing complex inventory systems. This reallocation of labor leads to higher productivity and better use of human capital, resulting in more strategic and impactful operations.

To illustrate the benefits of the Pudu D7, several industries have already seen measurable improvements in both cost savings and efficiency. In the restaurant industry, for example, restaurants that have integrated the Pudu D7 into their operations have reported significant labor cost reductions during peak service times. By automating the delivery of food and drinks, these establishments have been able to maintain a high level of service with fewer staff members, especially during busy periods. This has not only saved on labor expenses but also allowed restaurant staff to provide a more attentive and personalized customer service experience, leading to increased customer satisfaction and higher revenue.

In one case study from a popular chain of restaurants, the introduction of the Pudu D7 resulted in a 25% reduction in labor costs during lunch and dinner rush hours. The robot seamlessly took over the role of delivering meals to tables, allowing waitstaff to focus on upselling, handling customer requests, and managing larger sections of the restaurant. This automation not only improved the restaurant's operational flow but also led to higher table turnover, increasing the number of customers served during peak hours.

In healthcare, hospitals that have adopted the Pudu D7 for supply transport and medication delivery have also seen notable improvements in efficiency and cost reduction. A case study from a mid-sized hospital showed that by using the Pudu D7 to transport medical supplies and equipment across various departments, the hospital was able to save 15% on labor costs associated with routine supply runs. The robot's precision and ability to navigate busy hospital corridors allowed medical staff to focus more on patient care rather than being tied up with logistical tasks. Additionally, the hospital reported fewer delays in the delivery of time-sensitive materials, which contributed to better overall patient outcomes and a more streamlined workflow.

In retail, the Pudu D7 has been instrumental in increasing inventory management efficiency. A large retail chain that implemented the robot for shelf restocking and inventory tasks saw a 20% improvement in stocking speed. The robot's ability to quickly and accurately place items on shelves reduced the need for multiple workers to handle restocking duties, especially during off-peak hours. This allowed the store to allocate more workers to customer-facing roles, improving customer service and driving higher sales. Moreover, the robot's reliability in handling delicate or high-value products ensured that errors, such as damaged goods or misplaced inventory, were significantly reduced, leading to cost savings in shrinkage and product losses.

These case studies highlight the tangible benefits of integrating the Pudu D7 into various industries. The ability of the robot to automate routine tasks not only reduces operational costs but also increases efficiency, allowing human workers to be more productive and focused on strategic initiatives. In every case, the Pudu D7 has proven to be a valuable tool in enhancing business operations, whether by improving customer satisfaction, speeding up workflows, or minimizing costly errors. As industries continue to seek ways to optimize their operations, the Pudu D7's role in reducing costs and increasing efficiency will likely expand further, making it a vital component of modern business strategy.

Chapter 8: A Vision of the Future – Pudu's Roadmap

Pudu Robotics has a broad and ambitious vision: to create an ecosystem of robots that seamlessly integrate into various industries, each tailored to handle specific tasks and needs. This vision encompasses a range of robots, from specialized machines designed for highly specific functions to semi-humanoid robots like the Pudu D7, and even fully humanoid robots that are still on the horizon. By developing robots that can complement each other and work in harmony with human workers, Pudu Robotics aims to reshape the way businesses operate, increasing efficiency, reducing costs, and enhancing overall service delivery across multiple sectors.

The Pudu D7 represents a key part of this vision, standing as a semi-humanoid robot that blends the best of human-like capabilities with the practicality of task-specific machines. Semi-humanoid robots like the D7 are designed to bridge the gap between simple, highly specialized robots—such as those used solely for tasks like food delivery or cleaning—and the more complex, fully humanoid robots that are still in the early stages of development. The D7's adaptability, combined with its semi-humanoid design, makes it versatile enough to perform a wide range of tasks in environments that demand both precision and flexibility. This versatility is crucial in industries such as healthcare, hospitality, and retail, where the robot must seamlessly interact with both humans and objects in complex, dynamic spaces.

In this broader ecosystem, specialized robots are designed to handle routine, repetitive tasks efficiently. These robots are typically focused on a single function, such as food delivery or cleaning, and are programmed to perform these tasks with consistency and accuracy. While they are highly effective at what they do, their capabilities are limited when compared to semi-humanoid robots like the Pudu D7, which can learn, adapt, and perform a wider variety of functions. Fully humanoid robots, on the other hand, are envisioned to be capable of mimicking nearly all human movements and interactions, but their development is still in the experimental phase due to the complexities involved in creating machines that can replicate human dexterity and problem-solving abilities at scale.

Semi-humanoid robots like the Pudu D7 represent a sweet spot in this robotic ecosystem. They are advanced enough to take on complex, multi-faceted roles, but not as costly or challenging to implement as fully humanoid robots. As Pudu Robotics continues to innovate, the D7 and other semi-humanoid robots will play an increasingly vital role in shaping how businesses operate. The future of service robotics is not about replacing human workers entirely but augmenting human capabilities. Robots like the Pudu D7 can take over repetitive, physically demanding, or high-precision tasks, allowing human employees to focus on strategic, creative, and customer-facing roles that require emotional intelligence and decision-making.

This shift toward a more collaborative work environment, where robots handle the routine and humans manage the strategic, is already beginning to take shape. In the hospitality industry, for instance, semi-humanoid robots like the Pudu D7 are being deployed to handle guest services, food delivery, and luggage transport, all while interacting naturally with customers. In healthcare, these robots are taking on more responsibilities for tasks such as medication delivery, patient assistance, and logistical support, freeing up healthcare professionals to focus on critical care and patient interaction.

The future of service robotics, as envisioned by Pudu Robotics, will be characterized by this synergy between robots and human workers. As businesses continue to evolve and seek ways to improve efficiency, reduce costs, and enhance customer experiences, semi-humanoid robots like the Pudu D7 will become indispensable tools. They offer the perfect balance of adaptability, affordability, and capability, enabling them to fit seamlessly into a variety of roles across industries. Whether it's assisting in a hospital, working in a restaurant, or managing inventory in a retail store, the Pudu D7 and its successors will continue to shape the way we think about service work, automation, and the future of labor.

In this vision, robots are no longer just tools—they are collaborators, working alongside human employees to create more efficient, reliable, and dynamic business operations. The ecosystem that Pudu Robotics is developing, which includes specialized robots for single tasks, semi-humanoids like the D7, and eventually fully humanoid robots, will ensure that businesses have access to a range of robotic solutions tailored to their specific needs. This integrated approach will not only drive cost savings and operational improvements but will also unlock new possibilities for how work is done in the 21st century.

Pudu Robotics has set its sights on fully commercializing the Pudu D7 by 2025, a move that is poised to bring this advanced robot into a wider array of industries and everyday business operations. This commercialization plan represents a key milestone in Pudu's broader vision of integrating semi-humanoid robots into various sectors where efficiency, adaptability, and precision are critical. By 2025, the Pudu D7 will no longer be a specialized tool used in select environments—it will become a mainstream solution, accessible to businesses of all sizes looking to streamline operations, reduce costs, and enhance the customer or client experience.

The timeline for this full-scale commercialization reflects Pudu Robotics' commitment to refining the D7's capabilities and ensuring that it can seamlessly integrate into different industry settings. Over the next couple of years, the company will continue to develop and test the robot in diverse environments, ranging from restaurants and hospitals to retail stores and warehouses. By gathering data and refining the robot's performance based on real-world use cases, Pudu aims to ensure that the D7 is fully optimized for a broad range of applications by the time it is widely released.

Once commercialized, the Pudu D7 has the potential to revolutionize service industries on a global scale. As businesses continue to adopt automation and AI-driven solutions, the demand for robots that can perform complex, adaptive tasks—like those managed by the Pudu D7—will only grow. The robot's versatility means it can function in a multitude of roles, making it attractive to industries that value both precision and flexibility. Whether it's navigating a crowded restaurant floor or efficiently transporting medical supplies in a hospital, the Pudu D7's ability to adapt to different tasks and environments will make it an invaluable asset in the future of service robotics.

The potential for more advanced robots beyond the D7 is also part of Pudu Robotics' long-term vision. With advancements in AI, machine learning, and robotics technology, we can expect future iterations of the Pudu D7 and other robots in the Pudu lineup to become even more intelligent, capable, and versatile. These robots will not only perform routine tasks but may also begin to take on roles that require higher levels of decision-making, problem-solving, and interaction with humans. As AI models continue to evolve, robots like the D7 could learn to handle more sophisticated tasks, such as customer support, inventory management, or even assisting with complex procedures in medical and industrial environments.

Pudu Robotics' commitment to innovation suggests that by 2025 and beyond, we may also see an expansion of robots into industries that have yet to fully embrace automation. Fields such as logistics, manufacturing, and even education could benefit from robots that combine semi-humanoid features with the ability to learn and adapt. The Pudu D7's flexible design allows for further enhancements and customizations, meaning that future versions of the robot could be tailored to the specific needs of these industries. For example, in logistics, a more advanced Pudu robot might assist in warehouse management, sorting, and transporting goods in real time, while in education, robots could help with administrative tasks or even assist teachers in the classroom.

As Pudu Robotics works toward the full commercialization of the D7, the company is also laying the groundwork for broader applications of service robotics across multiple sectors. The next generation of robots will likely be more than just tools; they will become integrated parts of the workforce, capable of performing tasks that require intelligence, adaptability, and interaction. This shift could redefine the future of work, particularly in industries that rely on efficiency, precision, and customer service.

By 2025, with the full commercialization of the Pudu D7, we can expect robots to become an even more common sight in our everyday lives. The advancements that Pudu Robotics is pursuing not only signal a future where robots handle routine tasks with ease but also one where they enhance human productivity by collaborating in more strategic and impactful ways. As industries continue to evolve and adopt new technologies, robots like the Pudu D7 will play a crucial role in shaping how businesses operate and how human workers interact with intelligent machines.

The commercialization of the Pudu D7 marks just the beginning of a new era in service robotics. As these robots become more sophisticated and widespread, the possibilities for their applications are virtually limitless. Whether it's in healthcare, hospitality, retail, logistics, or even beyond, the Pudu D7—and future robots like it—will be at the forefront of this technological revolution, offering businesses a powerful tool to enhance efficiency and reduce operational costs while improving overall service quality.

Chapter 9: Technical Mastery – The Engineering Behind the D7

The Pudu D7 is engineered for long-lasting, uninterrupted operation, making it a highly reliable asset for industries that require continuous service. One of its key features is its impressive battery life, which allows it to operate for more than 8 hours without requiring downtime for recharging. This extended battery capacity is crucial for environments like hospitals, restaurants, and retail spaces, where tasks need to be performed consistently throughout the day or night. By ensuring long-lasting performance, the Pudu D7 minimizes disruptions in service and reduces the need for frequent human intervention to monitor or recharge the device.

The sustainability of this battery life is especially valuable in fast-paced settings where reliability is paramount. In a restaurant, for example, the Pudu D7 can work through an entire dinner service, delivering meals and handling customer interactions without needing to be taken offline for recharging. In hospitals, where the transport of medical supplies and equipment must happen efficiently and without delay, the robot's extended battery life ensures that it can work around the clock, assisting healthcare professionals without requiring frequent breaks. This reliability helps optimize operational workflows by reducing downtime, leading to greater productivity and improved service.

Beyond its impressive battery life, the Pudu D7 is equipped with advanced technical components that ensure both efficiency and versatility. The power system at the heart of the robot is designed to maximize energy efficiency while delivering consistent performance. This system not only supports the robot's mobility and functionality but also helps prolong the battery life by managing power consumption intelligently. For instance, the robot adjusts its energy usage based on the task at hand—whether it's navigating a complex environment or carrying out a more energy-intensive activity like lifting and transporting items.

The control mechanisms of the Pudu D7 are equally sophisticated, allowing the robot to operate with precision in real-time. These mechanisms are powered by an AI-driven system that handles both high-level planning and low-level task execution. High-level control planning enables the robot to make strategic decisions about its movements, routes, and task prioritization, while low-level control mechanisms ensure that each action—whether it's gripping an object or navigating around obstacles—is executed with accuracy and precision. This dual control system allows the robot to adapt to its environment and maintain optimal performance regardless of the challenges it faces.

The omnidirectional wheelbase, powered by the robot's control system, allows for seamless 360-degree movement. This component is crucial in environments where tight navigation is required, such as crowded hospital corridors or restaurant dining areas. The precision in its mobility ensures that the robot can maneuver efficiently, even in confined spaces, without sacrificing speed or stability. Additionally, the Pudu D7 is equipped with advanced sensors that allow it to detect and avoid obstacles in real-time, further enhancing its ability to operate autonomously in dynamic settings.

The adaptability of the Pudu D7 extends to its flexible arms, which are designed to handle a variety of attachments, from basic tools to humanoid hands. Each arm has 30 degrees of freedom, allowing the robot to perform complex tasks that require a range of motion. The arms are driven by a precise control system that enables the robot to handle delicate items or lift heavier loads with the same level of care and accuracy. Whether it's picking up fragile medical instruments in a hospital or restocking items in a retail store, the robot's control system ensures that each task is carried out with minimal risk of error.

Another key technical feature of the Pudu D7 is its hierarchical intelligence system, which combines AI, machine learning, and real-time data processing to enhance its adaptability. This system is responsible for the robot's ability to learn from its environment and refine its performance over time. By processing data from its sensors and interactions, the robot continuously improves its decision-making and task execution, making it more efficient with each use. The ability to learn and adapt not only enhances the robot's immediate performance but also ensures that it remains valuable in the long term as it evolves to meet the changing needs of its environment.

In terms of overall sustainability, the Pudu D7's efficient power consumption and long battery life contribute to reducing the environmental impact of automation. By operating for extended periods without needing frequent recharging, the robot helps businesses lower their energy consumption. Additionally, the design of the robot prioritizes durability, meaning it is built to withstand the demands of daily use in high-stress environments, reducing the need for frequent maintenance or replacement. This sustainability factor makes the Pudu D7 an attractive option for companies looking to reduce their operational costs while maintaining a commitment to environmentally friendly practices.

In summary, the Pudu D7's long battery life, advanced power systems, and intelligent control mechanisms make it a standout in the world of service robotics. Its ability to operate continuously for over 8 hours, combined with its precise control systems and adaptability, ensures that it can handle a wide range of tasks with minimal downtime. As industries continue to move towards automation, the Pudu D7's technical capabilities will allow businesses to optimize their operations efficiently, sustainably, and reliably.

Pudu Robotics' impressive portfolio of nearly 1,000 authorized patents underscores the company's commitment to cutting-edge innovation in the field of robotics. These patents reflect the extensive research and development (R&D) efforts that have gone into creating highly sophisticated robots like the Pudu D7. Each patent represents a unique technological advancement, covering various aspects of robotics, from AI-driven decision-making systems to mechanical design elements like omnidirectional mobility and adaptive arms. This breadth of intellectual property allows Pudu Robotics to stay ahead of the competition, continuously refining its products to meet the evolving demands of industries such as healthcare, hospitality, retail, and logistics.

The significance of these patents lies not only in the sheer number but also in the variety of technologies they cover. Pudu Robotics has developed innovations across the entire robotics ecosystem, including AI, machine learning algorithms, sensor technology, control systems, battery efficiency, and mechanical design. These patented technologies allow Pudu to enhance the versatility and functionality of its robots, making them adaptable to a wide range of tasks and environments. For example, patents related to the Pudu D7's omnidirectional wheelbase and precision arms ensure the robot's ability to move fluidly through tight spaces while performing intricate tasks that require dexterity. This kind of patented innovation sets Pudu Robotics apart as a leader in service robotics, continually pushing the boundaries of what robots can achieve.

Research and development have been the backbone of Pudu Robotics' success, driving continuous innovation and breakthroughs in robotic technology. The Pudu D7, for example, is the result of years of meticulous research, combining the latest advances in artificial intelligence, machine learning, and engineering. Pudu Robotics invests heavily in R&D, with teams dedicated to exploring new technologies, refining existing systems, and testing prototypes in real-world environments. These efforts ensure that each iteration of their robots is more advanced, reliable, and efficient than the last. For the Pudu D7, this commitment to R&D has led to a robot that can adapt to complex environments, learn from its interactions, and perform a variety of tasks with precision and accuracy.

One of the key areas where research and development have contributed to the Pudu D7's innovation is in its AI-driven decision-making capabilities. The robot's ability to learn and adapt in real-time is a direct result of advanced AI research, which allows it to process data from its environment, make decisions, and improve its performance over time. This AI-driven adaptability is essential in industries like healthcare and hospitality, where the environment is constantly changing, and the robot must be able to adjust its actions based on new inputs. Without the extensive

R&D efforts that go into refining these algorithms, the Pudu D7 wouldn't have the sophisticated decision-making abilities that make it stand out in the market.

A detailed look at the engineering challenges that Pudu Robotics has overcome reveals just how complex creating a robot like the Pudu D7 truly is. One of the primary challenges has been designing a robot that can navigate and perform tasks in diverse, real-world environments. The Pudu D7's omnidirectional wheelbase, for instance, required significant engineering innovation to ensure that the robot could move smoothly and precisely in crowded or tight spaces, such as busy restaurant floors or narrow hospital corridors. Engineering a wheelbase that allows for 360-degree movement without sacrificing speed or stability was a breakthrough in robot mobility, giving the Pudu D7 the flexibility needed to excel in environments where traditional robots would struggle.

Another major engineering challenge involved developing the robot's arms, which offer 30 degrees of freedom and can be equipped with various attachments, including humanoid hands. Designing these arms required overcoming significant mechanical and control system challenges to ensure that the robot could handle delicate objects with precision while also being strong enough to lift heavier items. The breakthrough in arm design, paired with advanced control mechanisms, enables the Pudu D7 to perform tasks that require both dexterity and strength, from delivering meals to transporting medical equipment.

Battery life and power management also posed a substantial engineering challenge. To meet the demands of industries that require long hours of uninterrupted service, Pudu Robotics needed to develop a power system that could support extended operation without sacrificing performance. The Pudu D7's battery system, which allows it to operate for more than 8 hours, is the result of extensive research into energy efficiency and sustainable design. Balancing power consumption with performance was a key breakthrough, ensuring that the robot could handle demanding tasks without frequent downtime for recharging.

In addition to these mechanical and power-related challenges, Pudu Robotics has also made significant breakthroughs in sensor technology and real-time adaptability. The Pudu D7's ability to navigate its environment autonomously relies on a complex network of sensors that allow it to detect obstacles, map its surroundings, and make real-time adjustments. Engineering these sensors to work seamlessly with the robot's AI and control systems required overcoming significant hurdles in data processing and integration. The result is a robot that can move autonomously through complex environments, making split-second decisions to avoid collisions or optimize its path.

The nearly 1,000 patents held by Pudu Robotics are a testament to the company's relentless pursuit of innovation. Each breakthrough in AI, mobility, dexterity, and power management contributes to making the Pudu D7 one of the most advanced service robots on the market. The company's commitment to research and development ensures that its robots will continue to evolve, meeting the growing demands of industries that require automation, precision, and reliability. As Pudu Robotics pushes the boundaries of what robots can achieve, the Pudu D7 stands as a prime example of how R&D drives both technological advancement and real-world applications.

Chapter 10: The Future of Human-Robot Collaboration

As semi-humanoid robots like the Pudu D7 become more integrated into industries, they will coexist with human employees in a way that enhances productivity and optimizes workflows, rather than replacing human roles entirely. These robots are designed to complement human labor by handling routine, physically demanding, or repetitive tasks, allowing human workers to focus on more strategic and creative endeavors. The relationship between robots and humans in the workplace will evolve into one of collaboration, where each plays a distinct role in the overall efficiency of the operation.

In industries such as healthcare, hospitality, and retail, semi-humanoid robots like the Pudu D7 are poised to become active participants in daily operations. Their ability to interact naturally with their environment and perform tasks that require precision and adaptability makes them invaluable assets. For example, in a hospital, the Pudu D7 can take over tasks like delivering medical supplies, navigating patient rooms, and assisting with logistical needs, freeing healthcare professionals to dedicate their time and energy to direct patient care. In this sense, the robot becomes a co-worker rather than just a tool, playing a supportive role in enhancing the overall efficiency of the hospital.

The key to this coexistence lies in how semi-humanoid robots can take on repetitive and physically exhausting tasks that humans may find draining, such as transporting items, delivering goods, or restocking shelves. This allows human employees to apply their unique skills—such as problem-solving, customer interaction, and critical thinking—to tasks that truly require human attention. By removing the burden of mundane tasks, robots like the Pudu D7 help improve the quality of work life for employees, enabling them to focus on tasks that are more rewarding and impactful.

What makes semi-humanoid robots distinct from more specialized machines is their ability to adapt and learn, which fosters a collaborative working environment. As participants in the workforce, robots like the Pudu D7 are not simply following pre-programmed instructions; they are evolving with each interaction, learning how to navigate new challenges, optimize their tasks, and improve efficiency over time. This adaptive intelligence allows them to work alongside human employees in dynamic environments where flexibility and quick decision-making are crucial.

In hospitality settings, for instance, the Pudu D7 can manage tasks like delivering room service or assisting with food service, tasks that often take up a large portion of staff time. By handling these routine duties, the robot allows human employees to concentrate on more complex interactions with guests, improving the overall quality of service. Robots become active collaborators in providing a seamless guest experience, taking over operational functions while employees can offer a more personalized and attentive service.

The integration of semi-humanoid robots into the workforce transforms them from simple tools into active participants in the business ecosystem. They are not static machines confined to a single task, but dynamic members of the team who can adjust to changing circumstances, making them highly valuable in environments where quick adaptation is required. Their ability to communicate with other machines, learn from human interactions, and contribute to the smooth operation of a business positions them as more than just automated systems—they are co-workers that help businesses operate more efficiently.

This shift also changes the way businesses think about automation. Instead of viewing robots as replacements for human jobs, they are now seen as enhancements to the workforce, helping to unlock new levels of productivity. The human workforce will remain crucial for tasks requiring emotional intelligence, complex decision-making, and creativity—areas where robots, even with advanced AI, cannot fully replicate human capabilities. Meanwhile, robots like the Pudu D7 can handle the physical, repetitive, and precision-based tasks that drain human resources, creating a balance that benefits both productivity and employee satisfaction.

As semi-humanoid robots continue to evolve, we are likely to see more industries embracing this partnership model, where robots and humans work side by side. These robots will not simply exist to execute tasks; they will become indispensable members of the workforce, contributing to the overall success of businesses by performing roles that complement human strengths. This new era of human-robot collaboration will redefine what it means to work efficiently, allowing businesses to harness the full potential of both human talent and robotic innovation.

As semi-humanoid robots like the Pudu D7 become more integrated into various industries, the emphasis on enhancing human-robot interaction is becoming central to improving both efficiency and customer satisfaction. The ability of robots to interact smoothly with human employees and customers in real-time is crucial to their effectiveness in service environments. By creating a seamless interface between human workers and robots, businesses can not only boost operational efficiency but also enhance the overall customer experience. Robots like the Pudu D7 are designed to work alongside humans, providing support in tasks that require precision and consistency, while freeing up human employees to focus on more complex and engaging duties.

In service-oriented industries like hospitality and retail, human-robot interaction directly impacts the quality of customer service. The Pudu D7, for example, can handle tasks like delivering food, guiding customers, or assisting with basic queries, ensuring that routine tasks are handled efficiently and consistently. This leaves human employees free to engage with customers more meaningfully, addressing their unique needs and concerns. When robots manage repetitive tasks, service speed increases, mistakes are minimized, and the overall flow of operations improves. The end result is a smoother, more responsive customer service process that enhances satisfaction and leaves a lasting positive impression.

In healthcare settings, enhancing human-robot interaction is particularly important for improving both patient care and the efficiency of hospital operations. Robots like the Pudu D7 can manage logistical tasks, such as delivering medical supplies or assisting with equipment, reducing the time nurses and doctors spend on these non-clinical duties. By doing so, healthcare professionals can devote more time and energy to patient care, enhancing the overall quality of the healthcare experience. The robot's ability to interact with staff seamlessly, adjusting its tasks based on real-time needs, ensures that operations flow smoothly without interruption, benefiting both patients and healthcare workers.

However, as robots become more integrated into workplaces, ethical considerations surrounding their use cannot be overlooked. One of the primary ethical concerns is the impact that increasing automation may have on jobs traditionally performed by humans. While robots like the Pudu D7 can significantly boost efficiency by taking over routine tasks, there is a valid concern that widespread automation could lead to job displacement in certain sectors. Businesses must balance the benefits of automation with the need to ensure that human workers are not unfairly marginalized. This requires careful planning and a commitment to upskilling and reskilling workers so that they can transition to roles that are better suited to human skills, such as decision-making, creativity, and emotional intelligence.

Another ethical consideration is the need for transparency in how robots are deployed and the data they collect. In many cases, robots are equipped with sensors and AI systems that allow them to gather information about their environment and interactions. Ensuring that these data-gathering processes are ethical and transparent is essential to maintaining trust between businesses, employees, and customers. Clear guidelines need to be in place to protect individual privacy and ensure that robots are not collecting or using data in ways that could infringe on personal rights or create uncomfortable working environments.

The humanization of robots also raises questions about how we interact with machines on a psychological level. As semi-humanoid robots become more advanced and capable of performing human-like tasks, there is a growing concern about how these machines should be treated and perceived in the workplace. Should robots be given a more personable identity to foster better interaction, or should they remain clearly distinct from humans to avoid confusion or unrealistic expectations? Striking the right balance between functionality and human-like qualities is important in ensuring that robots are effective without causing discomfort or misunderstanding among employees and customers.

Additionally, businesses must consider the ethical implications of how robots are integrated into customer-facing roles. While robots can significantly enhance service efficiency, they should not entirely replace human interaction in areas where personal connection is valued, such as hospitality and healthcare. Customers expect a level of empathy, warmth, and understanding from human staff, which robots are not yet fully capable of replicating. Therefore, robots should be used to complement human service, rather than replace it, ensuring that customer needs are met in a balanced way that preserves the human touch.

The integration of robots into the workforce also raises concerns about fairness and inclusivity. Businesses need to ensure that the introduction of robots does not disproportionately affect certain groups of employees, particularly those in lower-skilled jobs who may be more vulnerable to automation. It's crucial that organizations implement robots in a way that supports workforce development and creates new opportunities for all employees, rather than deepening social or economic inequalities.

In conclusion, while enhancing human-robot interaction can significantly improve efficiency and customer satisfaction, businesses must carefully consider the ethical implications of integrating robots into the workplace. Ensuring that robots complement rather than replace human workers, protecting privacy, and fostering inclusivity are all essential to maintaining a balanced, ethical approach to automation. By addressing these ethical considerations, businesses can fully realize the benefits of robotics while ensuring that their workforce and customers are treated with fairness and respect.

Conclusion

The Pudu D7 represents a transformative shift in how industries approach automation and service delivery. With its semi-humanoid design, advanced AI, and ability to adapt to dynamic environments, the Pudu D7 has proven to be an invaluable asset across industries such as healthcare, hospitality, retail, and more. Its capacity to handle a wide range of tasks, from delivering medical supplies to assisting customers, highlights its versatility and its potential to streamline operations while enhancing customer experiences. By taking over repetitive and physically demanding tasks, the Pudu D7 allows human workers to focus on more complex, strategic roles, ultimately improving both productivity and job satisfaction.

The Pudu D7 is more than just a service robot—it marks a significant evolution in the development of AI-powered machines. Where earlier robots were limited to performing highly specialized, task-specific roles, the Pudu D7's ability to learn, adapt, and evolve in real-time represents a new level of sophistication. Its multi-layered intelligence system, combined with advanced control mechanisms, allows it to function autonomously in complex environments, making it a key player in industries where flexibility and precision are essential. This evolution is a testament to the progress made in AI and robotics, with the Pudu D7 standing at the forefront of these technological advancements.

The introduction of the Pudu D7 into the workforce marks the beginning of a new era in service automation. It exemplifies how robots are no longer just tools but active participants in business operations. By integrating seamlessly into environments where human-robot interaction is critical, the Pudu D7 sets a new standard for what service robots can achieve. Its ability to handle a wide range of tasks with precision and reliability demonstrates how robots can enhance operational efficiency, reduce costs, and improve customer satisfaction. As industries continue to adopt automation, the Pudu D7 offers a glimpse into how AI-powered robots will become increasingly integrated into everyday business functions, reshaping how work is done across multiple sectors.

Looking ahead, the future for robots like the Pudu D7 is filled with possibilities. As AI technology continues to evolve, we can expect future iterations of the Pudu D7 to become even more intelligent, capable, and adaptable. Industries such as logistics, manufacturing, education, and even new fields will benefit from more advanced robots that can take on increasingly complex roles. The potential for robots to collaborate with human workers, rather than simply replacing them, opens the door to new forms of teamwork and efficiency, allowing businesses to achieve greater levels of innovation and productivity.

Beyond the Pudu D7, Pudu Robotics' vision of an ecosystem of robots—ranging from specialized machines to fully humanoid robots—signals that we are just beginning to unlock the potential of AI-powered automation. As these robots become more widespread, we are likely to see new applications emerge, from robots assisting in advanced medical procedures to managing complex supply chains. The integration of robots into more industries will undoubtedly shape the future of work, making human-robot collaboration a key aspect of business success.

In conclusion, the Pudu D7 is not just a technological innovation—it is a symbol of the future of service automation. It showcases how robots can enhance efficiency, improve customer experiences, and support human workers in meaningful ways. As we look forward, the advancements made with robots like the Pudu D7 will continue to push the boundaries of what is possible, heralding a new era where intelligent machines are essential partners in the modern workforce.

www.ingramcontent.com/pod-product-compliance
Lightning Source LLC
LaVergne TN
LVHW051713050326
832903LV00032B/4189